STOP PANIC ATTACKS

*Help Yourself Find Relief Without Medicine Pills
Attacking Anxiety Disorder Through Self Cures*

Descrierea CIP a Bibliotecii Naționale a României
FLETCHER, LISA
   Stop panic attacks : help yourself find relief without medicine pills : attacking anxiety disorder through self cures / By Lisa Fletcher. - București : My Ebook, 2018
   ISBN 978-606-983-610-1

159.9

STOP PANIC ATTACKS

HELP YOURSELF FIND RELIEF WITHOUT MEDICINE PILLS ATTACKING ANXIETY DISORDER THROUGH SELF CURES

My Ebook Publishing House
Bucharest, 2018

INTRODUCTION

I want to thank you and congratulate you for buying the book, "Stop Panic Attacks: Help Yourself Find Relief Without Medicine Pills – Attacking Anxiety Disorder Through Self Cures".

Having a panic attack can be quite scary. The good news however is that you are not alone. Each year, millions of Americans experience panic attacks. To be precise over 2 million Americans have a panic attack annually, with women being more likely to develop a panic attack compared to men.

While many people have a panic attack, this should not make you get comfortable and think that it is just a normal thing. The thing is that if you do not take the necessary steps to deal with panic attacks, you will become their slave and you will not achieve much in life. If you are tired of your panic attacks taking charge of your life, then this book is what you need.

This book is created as your ultimate guide to help you manage and overcome your panic attacks. In this book, you will learn about the symptoms of a panic attack so that you don't confuse it for a heart attack. You will also learn some quite effective strategies that if you implement will change your life and that you will effectively know what to do to overcome the panic attacks you frequently have. After reading this book, you will be empowered to take steps to stop panic attacks and life a better life.

Thanks again for purchasing this book, I hope you enjoy it!

Copyright 2018 – Zen Mastery, All rights reserved

This document is geared towards providing exact and reliable information in regards to the topic and issue covered. The publication is sold with the idea that the publisher is not required to render accounting, officially permitted, or otherwise, qualified services. If advice is necessary, legal or professional, a practiced individual in the profession should be ordered.

– From a Declaration of Principles which was accepted and approved equally by a Committee of the American Bar Association and a Committee of Publishers and Associations.

In no way is it legal to reproduce, duplicate, or transmit any part of this document in either electronic means or in printed format. Recording of this publication is strictly prohibited and any storage of this document is not allowed unless with written permission from the publisher. All rights reserved.

The information provided herein is stated to be truthful and consistent, in that any liability, in terms of inattention or otherwise, by any usage or abuse of any policies, processes, or directions contained within is the solitary and utter responsibility of the recipient reader. Under no circumstances will any legal responsibility or blame be held against the publisher for any reparation, damages, or monetary loss due to the information herein, either directly or indirectly.

Respective authors own all copyrights not held by the publisher.

The information herein is offered for informational purposes solely, and is universal as so. The presentation of the information is without contract or any type of guarantee assurance.

The trademarks that are used are without any consent, and the publication of the trademark is without permission or backing by the trademark owner. All trademarks and brands within this book are for clarifying purposes only and are the owned by the owners themselves, not affiliated with this document.

TABLE OF CONTENTS

Introduction 5

Chapter 1: KNOWLEDGE IS POWER–SYMPTOMS OF A PANIC ATTACK 13

Chapter 2: CONTROL YOUR BREATHING 19

Chapter 3: STOP RUNNING 24

Chapter 4: USE YOUR SENSES 28

Chapter 5: FOCUS ON OTHER THINGS 33

Chapter 6: PREPARE NOT TO PANIC 43

CONCLUSION 51

CHAPTER 1
KNOWLEDGE IS POWER: SYMPTOMS OF A PANIC ATTACK

Before you can find relief from panic attacks, you need to recognize when you're experiencing them in the first place. As we have said, many people treat panic attacks as heart attacks thanks to the conflicting symptoms. Such people rush (or are rushed to hospital) but by the time they get there, the panic attack may have run its course. Imagine their disbelief when the doctor tries to convince them that there is nothing wrong with their heart.

Yes, it is draining and depressing to experience such symptoms and although most symptoms exhibited when you are experiencing a panic attack will not land you in hospital, they can still be frightening.

But there's hope.

As they say, knowledge is power. Once you know what to expect, you can successfully turn things around and find relief from panic attacks. Some symptoms of a panic attack include:

- Chest pain
- Dizziness
- Racing heart
- Hyperventilation
- Emotional distress
- Sudden sweating
- Knot in the stomach
- A chocking feeling
- Fear of 'going crazy'
- Fear of dying

- Feeling detached or Derealization (being in a dream-like state)
- Nausea
- Trembling or shaking
- Feeling weepy
- Confusion
- An urgency to escape
- Feeling as if you're in danger

Of course, every person is different. You will not experience panic attacks in the same way someone else does. You may exhibit less or more symptoms. No matter, the symptoms you experience, it is critical that you recognize the symptoms.

Why is this important?

This is important because of the very nature of panic attacks. Let us put it this way. A panic attack starts with the release of adrenaline into your body. This is a natural response whenever the adrenal glands receive a message of fear. This message lets your adrenal glands know that there's an emergency and they should release adrenaline into your bloodstream so that you can either "fight or flee" from the emergency situation

It is very important to note that from the time your brain sends that emergency signal to your adrenal glands, it takes a mere 3 minutes for your body to become fully adrenalized. During this time, you will experience increased heart pumping and extra blood flow in your body.

Here's the catch.

As long as your adrenal glands keep receiving the emergency signal, they will continue releasing adrenaline into your bloodstream. All the while, your heart will be pumping faster and you will be experiencing other physical symptoms. In other words, you will be experiencing a panic attack.

Picture it this way. Your brain, for some unknown reason, starts sending emergency signals to your adrenal glands. Your adrenal glands start pumping adrenaline into your body so you can fight or flee a situation. However, you cannot do either because you have no idea where the emergency is, which means you are stuck in limbo.

As the seconds tick by, you become more anxious. You start panicking and your body continues releasing adrenaline making the symptoms worse. Frightful, isn't it? It does not have to be. Here is why.

Well, just as it takes 3 minutes for your body to become fully adrenalized, it also takes 3 minutes for your body to successfully stop releasing adrenaline. This means that if you react quickly, you can effectively stop panic attacks within 3 minutes. You just need to let your adrenal glands know that there is no emergency. Hence, there is no need to keep releasing adrenaline. Once you do this, the symptoms will fade.

But, how exactly can you do that? The subsequent chapters will elaborate how.

CHAPTER 2

CONTROL YOUR BREATHING

Runners breathe fast. They need to in order to keep up with their faster heart pumping. If you are not running, you do not need to breathe faster. Relax! Seriously, you need to slow down your breathing. If you continue breathing rapidly and shallowly, the only thing you will be doing is fueling the panic attack.

On the other hand, if you practice controlled breathing, you will normalize and even slow down your heart rate. You'll also help slow down the sweating and because you'll stop hyperventilating, you'll lower your blood pressure. Additionally, you will effectively reestablish control and this will play a major role in relieving your panic attack.

So, how should you go about it?

Once you notice the onset of a panic attack, the first thing you need to do is take a deep breath. Don't release it. Instead, hold the breath for as long as you can. This action will balance your levels of oxygen and carbon dioxide. As a result, it will reduce the feeling of being unable to breathe.

Once you have held that breath in for as long as you can, don't release it. Instead, breathe in slowly and then proceed to breathe out even more slowly. Continue this action of diaphragmatic breathing until you are in control of your breathing. If you're new to diaphragmatic breathing, there are some things you can do to practice this type of breathing. You should:

1: Sit on a chair

Find a comfortable chair to sit on. Sit down with your knees bent and with your shoulders and neck relaxed. Next, place one hand on your chest. Place your palm gently across your chest. Place the other hand just below your ribcage touching your stomach.

2: Breathe in slowly

Once your hands are in position, breathe in through your nose. Make sure you're breathing in slowly. During this time, you need to keep your chest still. The hand on your chest should not be moving. As you breathe in, you will notice that the hand on your stomach will move out. This is because your stomach will expand as you take in air.

3: Breathe out more slowly

Next, breathe out very slowly. As always, try to keep the hand on your chest from moving. As you exhale, you should be able to notice the hand on your stomach move back in as the air escapes.

Diaphragmatic breathing is a very potent way to deal with panic attacks. It lets your body know you are not in danger, which helps get rid of many of the symptoms associated with panic attacks. This is why you need to practice such breathing. This way, even if you have a panic attack, your 'muscle memory' will kick in to help bring your breathing back to normal.

During a panic attack, you can take diaphragmatic breathing a little further by using the 5-2-5 breathing method. This is where you inhale deeply for 5 seconds and then instead of exhaling, you hold your breath for 2 seconds. Finally, you exhale for a period of 5 seconds and repeat this sequence 5 times. Upon completing the sequence, your breathing should have normalized or even lowered.

What else can you do to stop a panic attack?

CHAPTER 3
STOP RUNNING

When you're in danger, your body produces adrenaline to give you the strength you need to fight or flee. This is a welcome reaction but an unnecessary one when you're not in danger. This is why you need not run during a panic attack.

There is more.

Your brain is very good at making associations. In fact, this may very well be the reason for panic attacks. This is because many of us can pinpoint certain 'triggers' that led to our panic attacks. Your brain 'sees' something and connects it to something else. It then quickly tells your adrenal glands to start producing adrenaline and before you know it, you start experiencing a full-blown panic attack.

If you notice the onset of a panic attack and you run, you are in essence telling your brain that it is right; you're reinforcing your fear because that surge in adrenaline has one purpose: help you fight or flee.

That's not all.

Once you run, your brain begins associating that place or that environment with danger. For example, if you have a panic attack while at a supermarket and you run, your brain stores that information. Thus, you may end up experiencing a panic attack whenever you visit a supermarket.

It won't stop there.

The supermarket has shoppers and it has items on the shelves. This means your brain may go further and start cross-associating people with danger. It may also associate other environments that 'look like a supermarket' with danger. Thus, you may end up panicked whenever you are around many people, whenever you enter a shop or supermarket, or even whenever you go to the library.

Because you are human, you may start dreading those places or situations. This will only reinforce your fear and lead to more panic attacks. This is why you need to stay where you are. Don't run. Instead, work to calm yourself down – you can try diaphragmatic breathing – while you're still in the same place.

This is important because for one, you'll be telling your brain that there is no emergency. Secondly, you will shift the focus from the place, as your brain will now know that the place is not dangerous.

If we go back to the supermarket example, once you have calmed down a bit, you should continue down the aisles checking out the products. Try to recall the location of specific items. Compare and contrast similar items and find new products that interest you.

The idea is to spend a bit more time in the place while you are relaxed so that your brain adjusts its thinking. Once you separate the panic attack from the place, you'll be less likely to experience an attack just because you happen to be in a similar location. This is a very good thing.

Now that you can't run, what can you actually do? Well, you can use your senses to control the situation. Here is how.

CHAPTER 4

USE YOUR SENSES

One important thing you need to note is that the flight or fight response is very physical in nature. How many times have we heard of people getting hurt because they were fleeing from something? If you are in a crowd and something happens, people start running. Many have no choice but to go with the flow lest they be trampled on. Others end up running towards the danger instead of away from it because they did not bother to identity where the danger was coming from.

To counteract such a physical response, you must engage your brain. Make it start thinking. You can do this by using your senses.

Use your eyesight

One of the symptoms of a panic attack happens to be "being in a dream-like state." Panic attacks try to take you away from reality. You must not let that happen. You must strive to remain in the present. You can do this by identifying 5 things you can actually see in your immediate surroundings.

Look at one thing, name it, look at another thing, name it and continue doing this until you have identified 5 things. This will change your perception. It will let your brain know that the situation is not one that calls for a surge of adrenaline.

When you see everyday things that you can name and associate with other things, you'll start differentiating between the dream-like state and reality.

Use your sense of touch

This next step requires you to use your sense of touch. The truth is that you touch many things throughout the day. Normally, this does not register unless the thing you touch leaves a mark on your hand.

This time, you will be deliberately touching things. You will be focusing your brain on what you are touching. Find 4 things you can touch and try to describe how they feel. Is what you are touching warm or cold, soft or rough? Keep your brain engaged in the activity so that it shifts its focus from the panic attack.

Listen

The environment is full of many wondrous sounds. You need to isolate the sounds and identity them until you can name at least 3 sounds. Do you hear music? Do you hear a child's laughter? Do you hear the sound of traffic? Identify and name those sounds.

When you are experiencing a panic attack, you may hear your heart beating. Do not dwell on this sound. In fact, deliberately listen to other sounds so that you can stop focusing on sounds associated with the panic attack.

Use your sense of smell

Another thing you can do is identify the smells in your surroundings. If you are near someone cooking, try to figure out what the person is cooking. If you are outside, try to figure out the smells that hit your sense of smell. Make it a point to identify at least 2 smells.

This will keep your mind busy. It will also slow down your breathing. This is because you actually have to put in effort to inhale deeply in order to capture the smells. You may actually have to breathe in a smell more than once as you try to identify it. Just remember to breathe out slowly after you do.

Taste

Don't forget to employ the sense of taste as you try to regain control. It may seem weird if you go about licking things but it's for a good cause; plus, you can be subtle about it. You can taste something you are carrying. You can taste the rain. You can taste samples of foodstuffs at a grocery store. You can go ahead and describe the taste. This will engage your mind. Try to taste 1 thing for this exercise.

Your senses are important. They can send powerful signals to the brain. They can let your brain know that everything is all right and that there is no need to panic. Use them. Use them to shift your focus. This will make it a lot easier to focus on other things.

CHAPTER 5
FOCUS ON OTHER THINGS

If you use any email service, you no doubt appreciate the trash function. Over the course of a week, tons of emails can find their way to your inbox. Once you sit down to review your email, you have the option to read the mails or trash them.

Now imagine you've subscribed to a certain blog and that this blog is advertising a certain course that's starting in a month's time. Because you are interested in the course, you mark the date on your calendar and eagerly await it.

What happens the next day? You get the same email reminding you of the course. In this case, you don't need to open the mail, you can trash it. After all, you already know its contents.

Panic attacks are like that reminder notification. They alert you to the fact that your body is very capable of producing adrenaline during an emergency. Do you need a constant reminder of that? The answer is no. You already know that. Thus, if your body is insistent on sending you such reminders, you need to trash them. Better still, you can change your 'subscription options' to stop your body from sending such messages.

How exactly can you go about this?

You can do this by focusing on something else. Here is the thing. When your body sends you an emergency message, quickly glimpse at it and determine whether it is an urgent message or just a reminder notification.

If it's a reminder notification or a panic attack, immediately start taking steps to send it to your mental trash box. In this case, you need to let it know that you acknowledge it but since you already know its content, you're placing it in the trash compartment by focusing on other things. There are various ways you can shift the focus. These include:

Count

If at the onset of a panic attack, you remember nothing else, remember to count. Let's put it this way. Your brain cannot count and panic at the same time. It can only do one or the other. You must impose your will on it so that it does the thing you want it to do: Start counting.

Make the exercise a bit more engaging for your brain by counting backwards in jumps of three. This will require a bit more concentration. It will keep your brain focused on numbers and allow the panic attack to fade away.

Call someone

You don't have to go through a panic attack by yourself. You can call someone else who is aware of the situation and who can help you calm down. Talk about it beforehand. This way, when you call the person, you won't have to bring up the topic. You can just go on and talk about something else.

Chew gum

Many people frown upon the action of chewing gum. However, many others will attest to its effectiveness at dealing with various issues. For example, those who want to quit smoking often replace that bad habit with chewing gum. Chewing gum can also help you eliminate symptoms such as nausea and others that crop up as you experience a panic attack. It also gives you an adrenaline outlet.

Recite the alphabet backwards

The alphabet is not something you think about often unless you have a child who is learning to read. The alphabet can come in handy when you are experiencing a panic attack. To calm yourself down, recite the alphabet backwards. Your brain will have no choice but to concentrate on the task simply because reciting the alphabet backwards is not common to it.

Play games on your phone

There are numerous phone games out there. You can have several games to suit your mood. You can also have phone games you turn to whenever you have a panic attack. Find a game that will engage you. It can be something as easy as arranging blocks. Block games are deceptively simple but they do require patience and concentration. By the time you have layered several blocks, you should have calmed down.

Play with a toy

Toys are not just for kids. They are for adults too. You can find relief from panic attacks by playing with an engaging toy. You can even bounce a ball about. Make the game engaging by aiming at a particular spot. This will ensure you keep your eyes on the ball. It will also make you move about and use that extra energy as you try to keep up with the bouncing ball.

Color

Coloring is another activity that can truly engage your brain. For this, you can use various adult coloring books and coloring apps. When coloring, you have to be careful not to color outside the designated lines. You also have to check that you're using the right colors. These activities ensure you focus on the coloring instead of the panic attack. Once you finish the picture, there is that satisfaction that comes from seeing the images you have colored.

Reread a book

Many fictional books take you to another world. They are an escape for many people and still, many others use books to relax. This is why it is common to hear people listing reading as a hobby. You can take advantage of books. You can use them to transport yourself from that undesired environment to an environment filled with hope and mystic.

You can have that go-to book that you know very well. Read a favorite passage from it and try to see it in a different light. When you start thinking of other things, you'll force your brain to focus on the new messages it is receiving. This will effectively remove the focus from a panic attack.

Watch a funny cartoon

There is always that one cartoon or comedy show that can make you laugh. Find it and use it whenever you need some help relaxing. Laughter, as they say, happens to be the best medicine. A funny cartoon takes you to that happy place, a place where panic attacks cannot exist. If you have Netflix, you can watch the cartoon right from your phone. If for some reason you cannot access a funny cartoon, there is nothing preventing you from thinking about it and even reciting some lines from it.

Visualize yourself doing yoga

Yoga is an activity that has the ability to relax you. You can use it to calm yourself. You do not need to actually engage in it at the time you sense a panic attack. You can just visualize yourself doing it. Start by imagining yourself changing into comfortable clothes. Next, picture yourself positioning the yoga mat and then doing some simple yoga poses. Since the best way to practice yoga poses is at a leisurely pace, if you picture yourself doing them, you'll start relaxing, which will stop your panic attack.

Make something

You don't need to have a 'creative bone' in order to make something. You can keep yourself occupied by indulging your imagination. If you like cooking, you can use that to calm yourself. Indeed, many people find cooking therapeutic. You can also find a hobby that calls for some creativity, or you can scrub the floor (if that makes you relax).

Alternatively, you can engage in any relaxing physical activity that allows you to use up the extra energy. At the end of it, you will end up with a clean home and that will make you feel good.

Talk yourself through it

Self-talk is a powerful tool. You can use it in a positive way to help you get through a panic attack. The first thing you need to remind yourself is that you are okay and that you are not in danger.

You can repeat a certain positive mantra until you're calm. Panic attacks, although scary, do not last forever. They can be over in minutes. You just have to remind yourself that.

You can do various things to shift the focus away from your panic attack. Find something that works for you and use it to calm yourself down. This will also make you better at preparing not to panic

CHAPTER 6
PREPARE NOT TO PANIC

Preparation is called the key to success for good reason. It gives you the tools you need to combat whatever situation you may find yourself in. When it comes to panic attacks, you should do your best to prepare not to have them. You should:

Know what to expect

This is a point we have already looked at but that needs repetition. You need to understand what panic attacks are. You need to know how to identify one and what symptoms you might experience. The more you know, the better you will be at pin pointing the start of a panic attack.

This means you can easily stop it within the first few minutes.

One way you can know more about panic attacks is by reading material on the subject. Another way is by recording your observations. As we have said, we are all different. We experience panic attacks differently. The best way to discover how panic attacks affect you is by monitoring and recording things such as dates, times, symptoms, and triggers. It is easier to know what triggers your panic attack. This is why you should try to note down your observations immediately. They will come in handy when you desensitize yourself.

Talk about it

It is not easy to talk about your fears. That said, there is something you need to know about your brain. Your brain thrives on imagination. If you allow certain thoughts to fester, your fear will grow larger. You will find yourself fearing panic attacks.

However, if you refuse to be silent, you will start seeing beyond your perception. Your thoughts will start arranging themselves. You will no longer remain stuck in a loop of fear. Talking about it also allows you to look at the situation objectively. Panic attacks alert you to perceived danger. If you start experiencing a panic attack, you need only to talk yourself through it by pointing out the reality of the situation.

You can also talk to others about the panic attacks. Use it as a teaching opportunity. This will make others aware of panic attacks. It will also reinforce the teachings. As you teach others about panic attacks, you will be cementing the knowledge in your own brain. This will change your perception and you will learn to recognize the signs and act quickly to stop the attack.

Adapt to triggers

If you want to adapt to triggers, you have to expose yourself to them. Some people recommend using a trained therapist for this exercise. The idea is to reenact similar scenes that cause you to go into a panic attack.

For example, some people experience panic attacks when they are feeling dizzy. In this case, they would have to make themselves dizzy on purpose to become familiar with the feeling. This is easy to accomplish by going round in circles. If you do this in a controlled environment, your body will learn that dizziness is no cause for panic.

Something else you can do is deliberately make your heart pump faster by jogging on the spot. Once you do this, use the diaphragmatic breathing techniques to slow down your breathing. The point of this exercise is to learn how to slow down your breathing quickly. As you recall, one of the first symptoms of a panic attack is your heart pumping faster. If you learn to control your breathing, you will learn to control panic attacks.

You can also visualize the situations that lead to a panic attack and then follow this with rehearsing your response. This mental rehearsal gives you a safe environment to think about the panic attacks and replace your response with calmness

Adopt a healthy lifestyle

Your health has a lot to do with your lifestyle. The foods you eat can lead to certain deficiencies that may trigger panic attacks. For this reason, you need to eat a balanced diet and ensure your body has all the vitamins it needs.

You also need to keep active during the day. Exercise is a good thing. It releases stress, which is a common panic attack trigger. If you are not used to exercise, ease into it. For example, you can walk for some time before you even try running.

Another thing you need to do is make sure you get enough sleep. Sleep debt is the root cause of various ailments including panic attacks. It causes things such as lack of focus, weak muscles, and headaches. These things can trigger panic attacks. Thus, if you improve your sleep pattern, you will in effect be doing away with many of the things that can trigger panic attacks.

If you wish to improve your sleep, you should find an appropriate sleep routine. Your routine should include your sleep time and a bunch of activities you will be doing to prepare for bed. You can include activities such as a warm bath and listening to soft music. You also need to determine when you will be waking up to ensure you get enough sleep. This will help you prevent panic attacks.

Live your life

Panic attacks should not take center stage in your life. They should not prevent you from fulfilling or living your dreams. This is why you should prepare to continue with your life even if you to happen to have a panic attack.

This means you should not shy away from places that could trigger an attack. Avoidance does not solve the problem. It just puts you in a box and makes your world smaller. As we have already stated, your brain is good at making associations. You must expose it to places it associates with fear and let it know that the reality is different from its perception.

If you start experiencing the symptoms of a panic attack, quickly start using the various techniques to calm yourself down. This will stop the panic attack from progressing. Once you've calmed down, continue what you were doing before. Slowly but surely, your panic attacks will lessen, and even if you were to have another attack unexpectedly, you will know exactly the steps you need to take to relieve it.

Overall, do not let panic attacks define you.

CONCLUSION

It's true that panic attacks can be frightening. Nevertheless, you have to stop looking at them like the enemy. When your body receives that emergency message, it starts releasing adrenaline to help you deal with whatever it is.

Adrenaline is not bad. However, when it is released continuously in the absence of an emergency, it becomes an issue. It is up to you to let your body know that there is no need to panic. You can do that by shifting your focus to something else. Therefore, go ahead and employ the various methods we've discussed here to find relief from panic attacks.

We have come to the end of the book. Thank you for reading and congratulations for reading until the end.

If you found the book valuable, can you recommend it to others? One way to do that is to post a review on Amazon.

Thank you and good luck!

Preview Of 'Anxiety Workbook'

This book has actionable information on how to manage, cope and overcome anxiety, cure phobia and reach mindfulness mastery.

We all have our moments when we are scared or afraid of the unknown. It is natural (survival) instinct for us humans to fear the unknown. We all love certainty. We love it if we could check all the boxes regarding anything we want. Whether it is speaking in public, meeting new people, heights, interviews etc.; we wish there could be a way in which we could get 'insider' information into the future so that we can prepare adequately. Unfortunately, as you are well aware, the future is very well known for its characteristic of being very uncertain. While the fear is often warranted, more often than not, the fear is completely unfounded but we just cannot seem to take charge of the situation.

For instance, we could simply be afraid of being in dark or enclosed places, afraid of speaking in public, meeting new people, afraid of heights, afraid of insects and many other things. What's strange is that most of us know that some of these fears are unfounded yet we cannot gather enough courage to overcome them; we are helpless. All this is anxiety and can have a profound negative effect in our lives. For instance, anxiety can make it hard for you to forego different opportunities e.g. new job opportunities, just because you are afraid of the unknown, anxiety can make you not interact with people as you would want to, can make it hard to quit a job that you distaste, can drain your energy and leave you feeling tired, etc. All these can make you feel disappointed with yourself in life and could ultimately bring such problems like low self-esteem, low self-confidence, mediocrity and much, much more.

Since you are reading this, it is clear that you want to do something about your anxiety. Lucky for you, this book has all you need to know to fight anxiety successfully so that you can unlock the opportunities that have been passing you by and transform your life in ways you've never imagined. In this book, you will learn to combat anxiety by following 7 simple steps. We will start by u understanding what anxiety is, as this helps you to know what you are up against, signs that you are suffering from anxiety, how to identify your fears, different methods through which you can fight anxiety, when you should seek professional help and much, much more!

Check out the rest of '*Anxiety Workbook: The Proven System for Managing, Coping and Overcoming Anxiety for Both Women & Men; Cure Your Phobia and Reach Mindfulness Mastery*' on Amazon.

www.ingramcontent.com/pod-product-compliance
Lightning Source LLC
Chambersburg PA
CBHW070950180426
43194CB00041B/2030